The Heather Doram
Caribbean Collection Coloring Book

ABOUT THE ARTIST

Heather Doram is a visual and performing artist
from the beautiful country of Antigua and Barbuda.
Her entire childhood was spent in the countryside;
where she always found joy and endless inspiration
in observing the flora, fauna, ocean, village life,
and people around her. She also creates art that
showcases her heritage and culture.

Her fanciful hand drawn illustrations will surely
bring joy, peace, colour and creativity to your life.
This collection invites you to explore her island
home and discover it's beauty along the way.

Find Heather on Facebook and IG @heatherdoramart

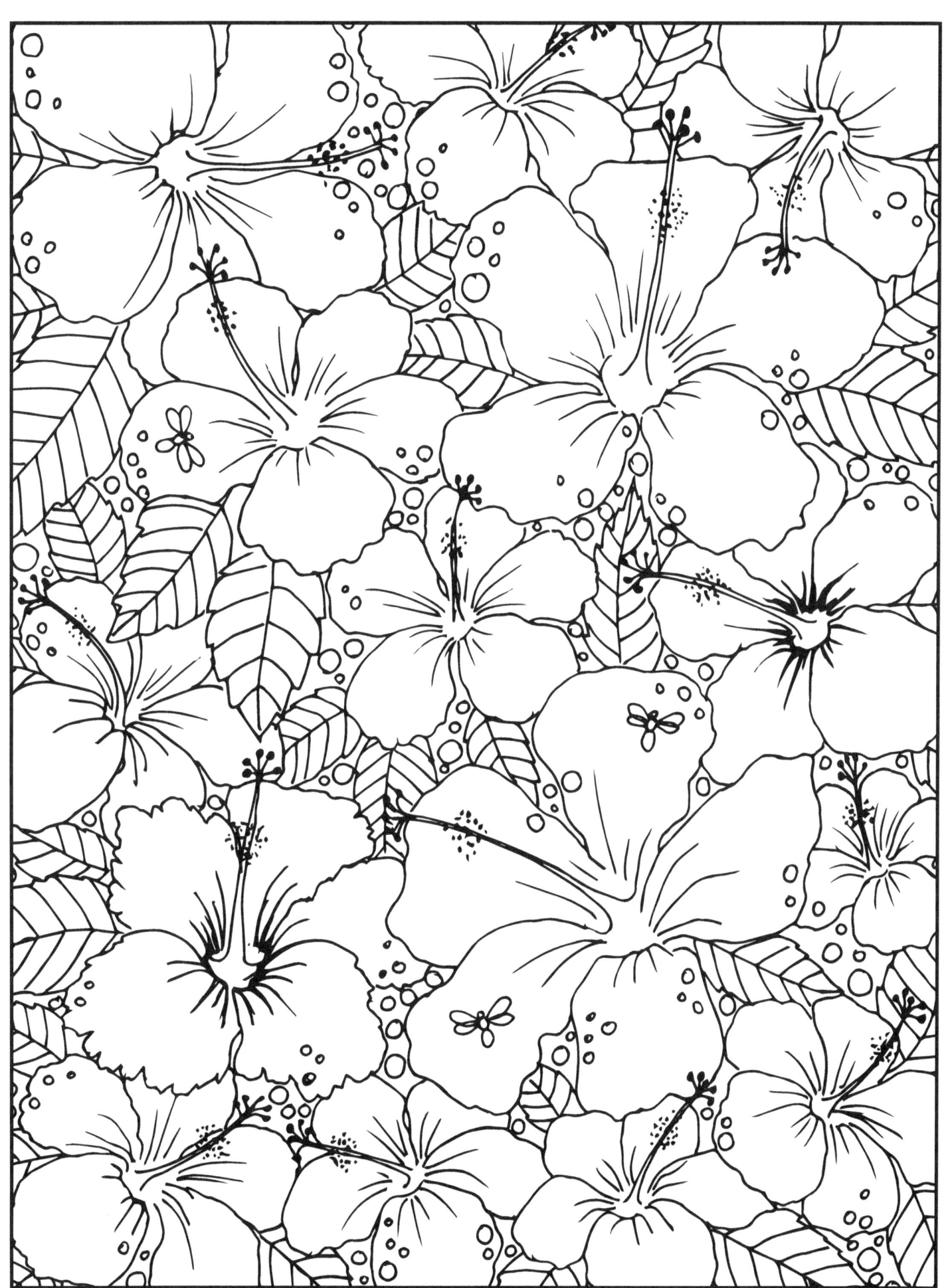

Caribbean Collection - NATURE

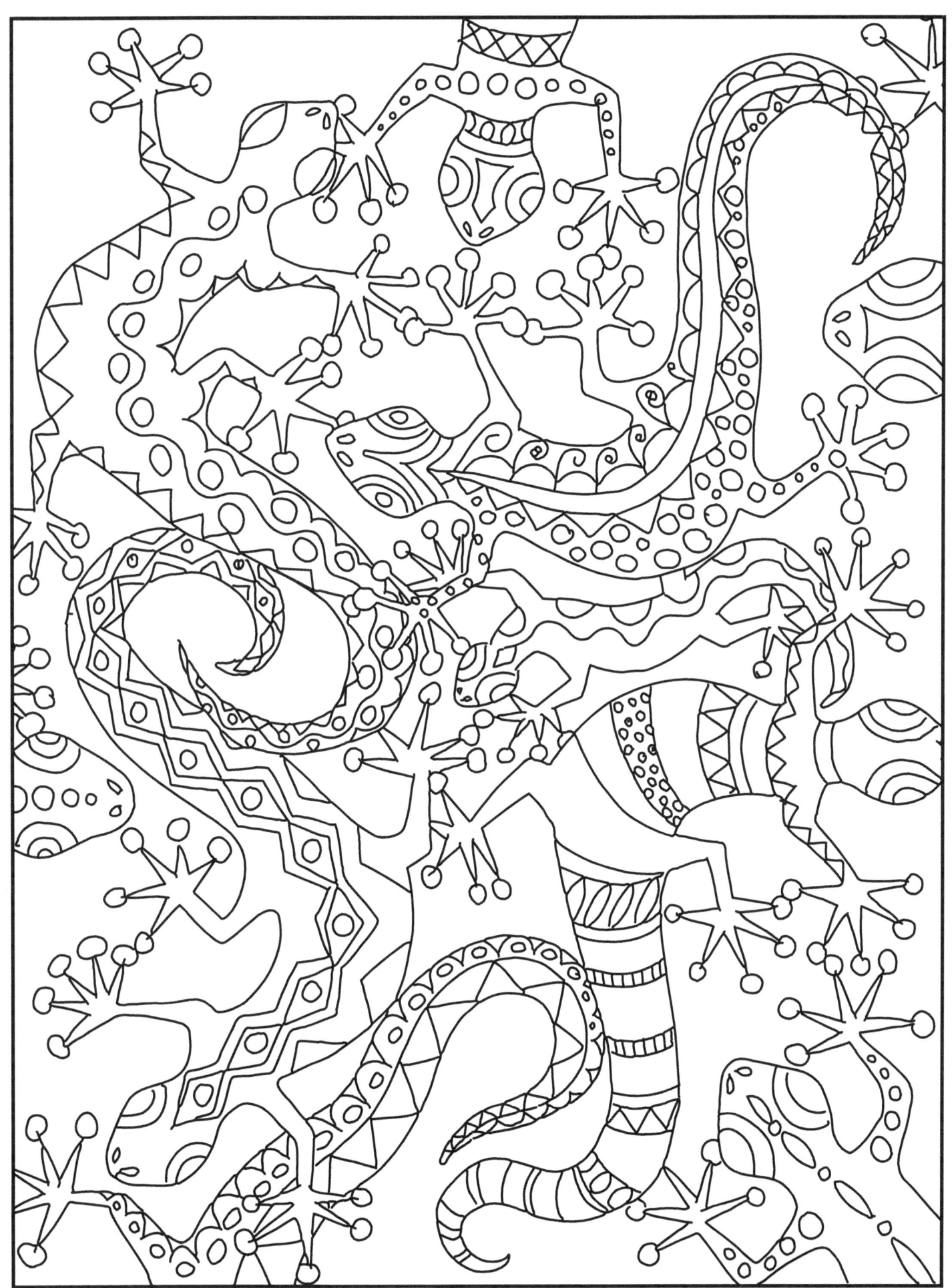

Caribbean Collection - NATURE

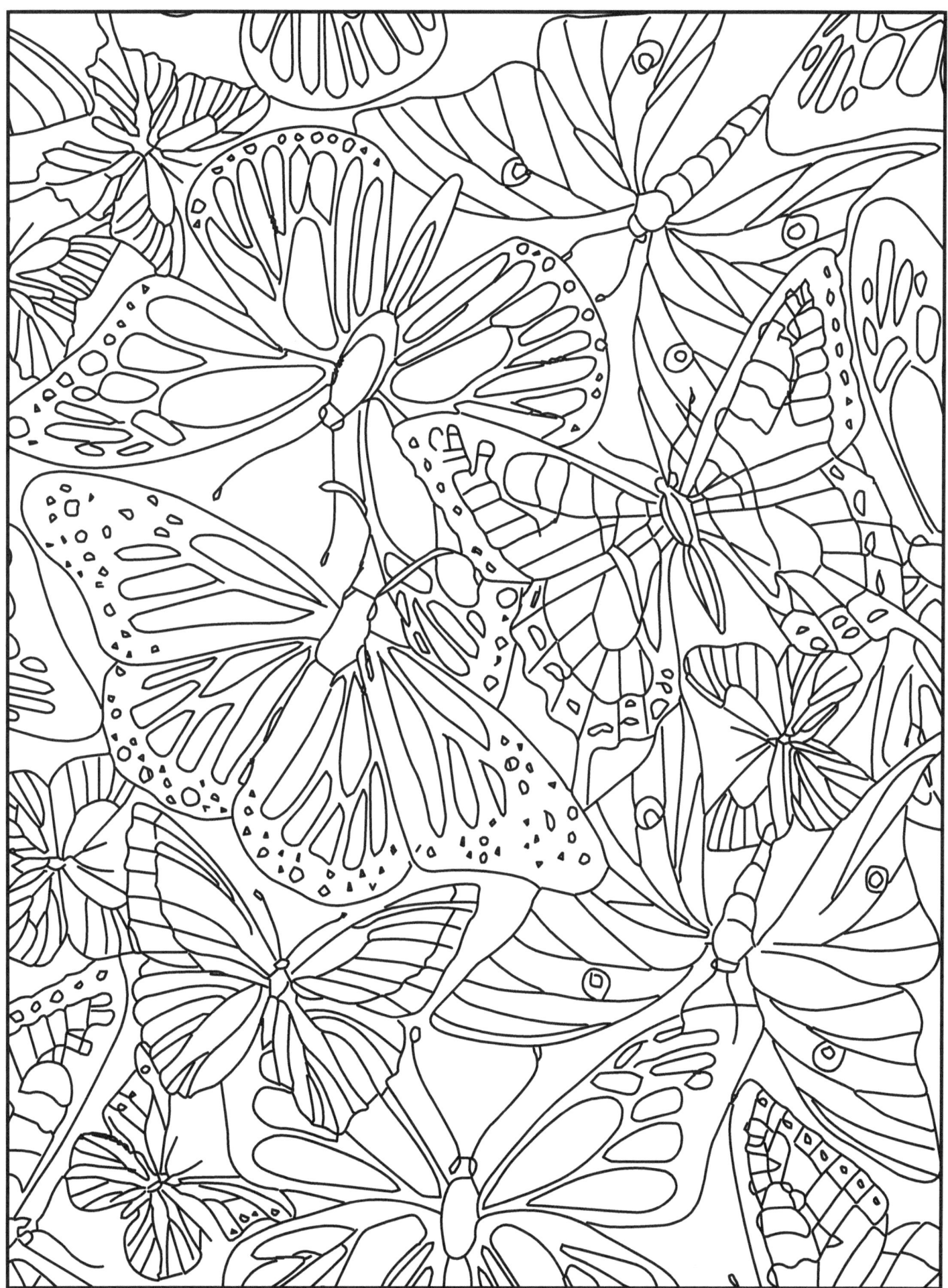

Caribbean Collection - NATURE

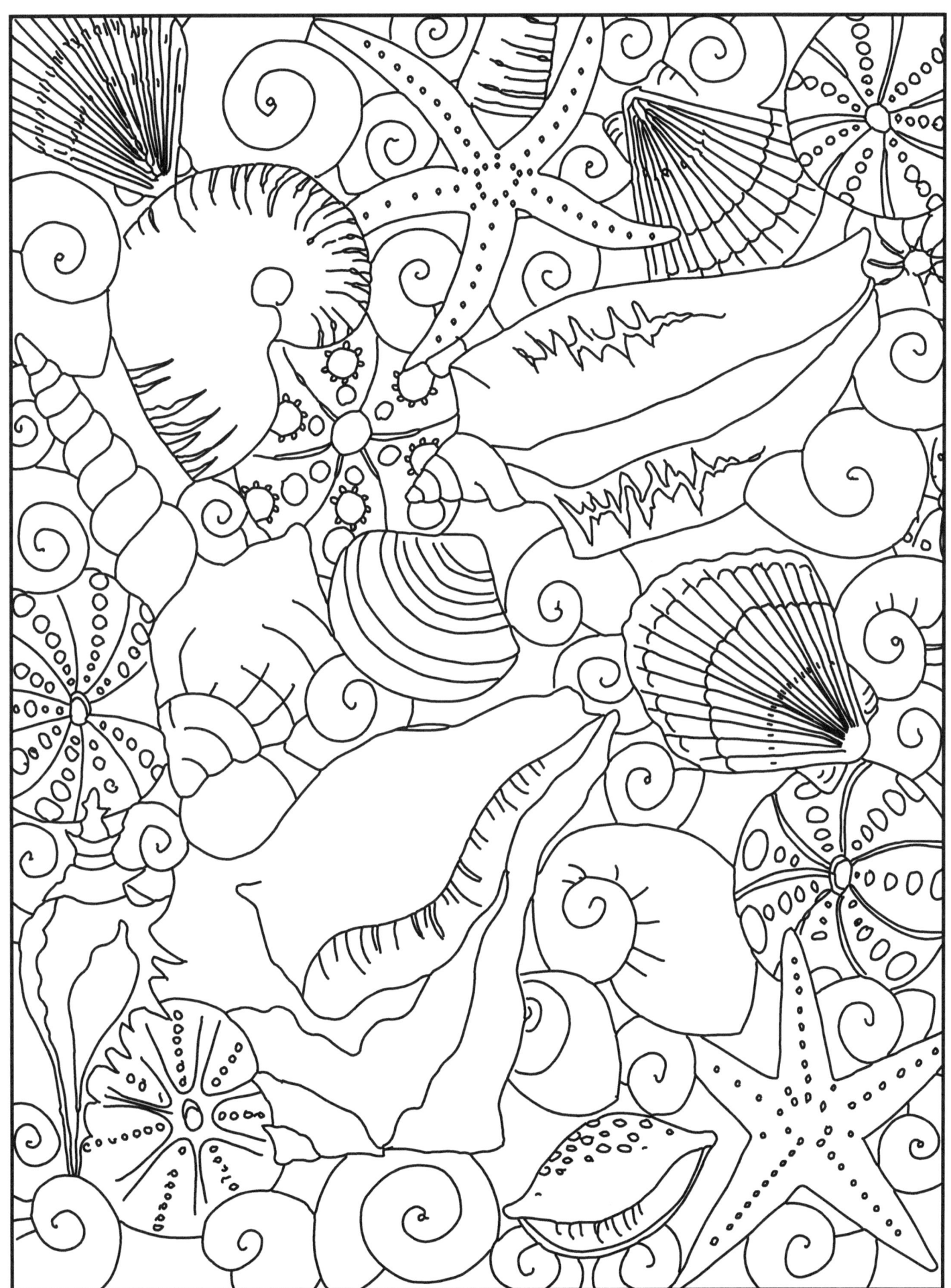

Caribbean Collection - NATURE

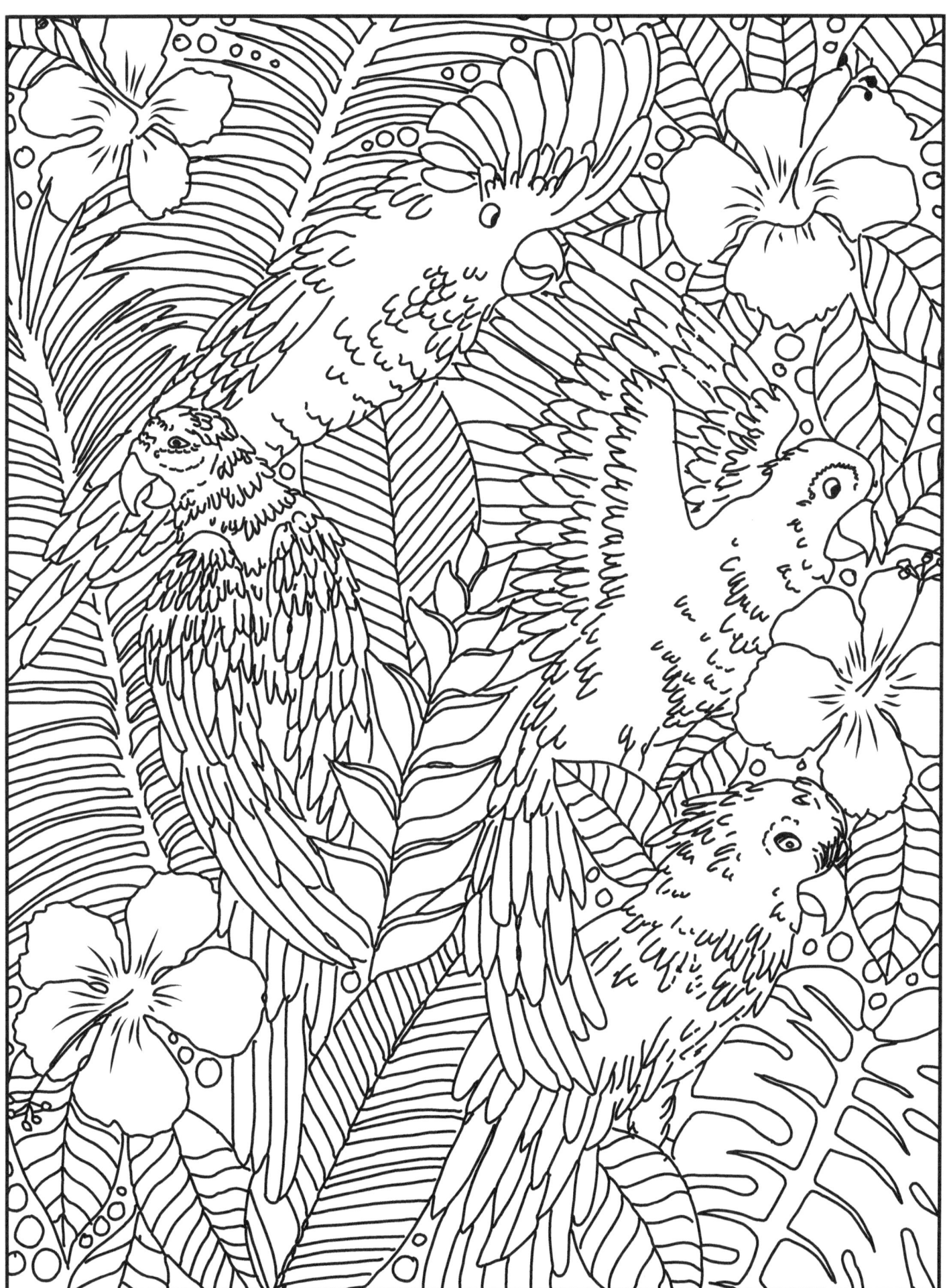

Caribbean Collection - NATURE

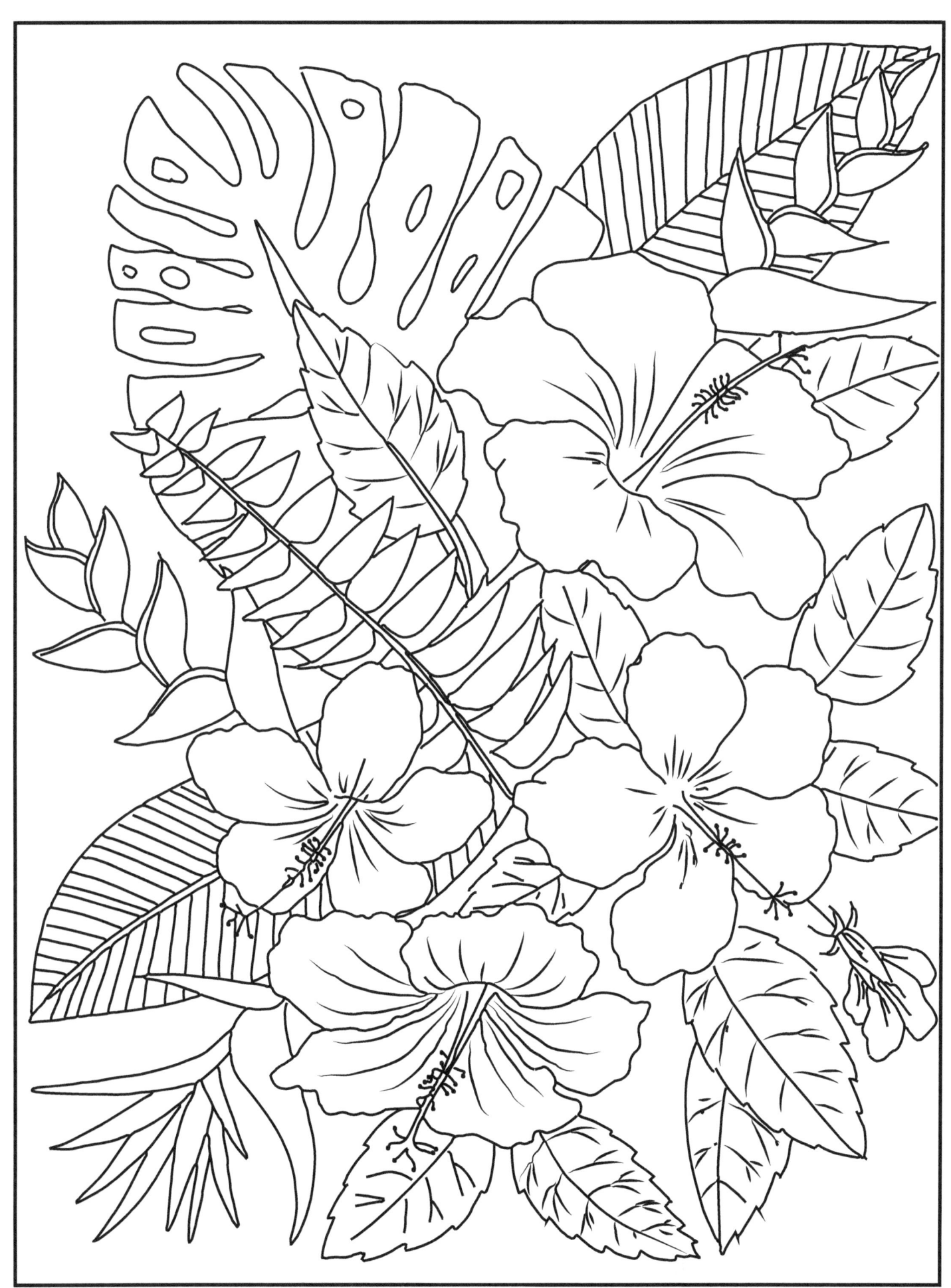

Caribbean Collection - NATURE

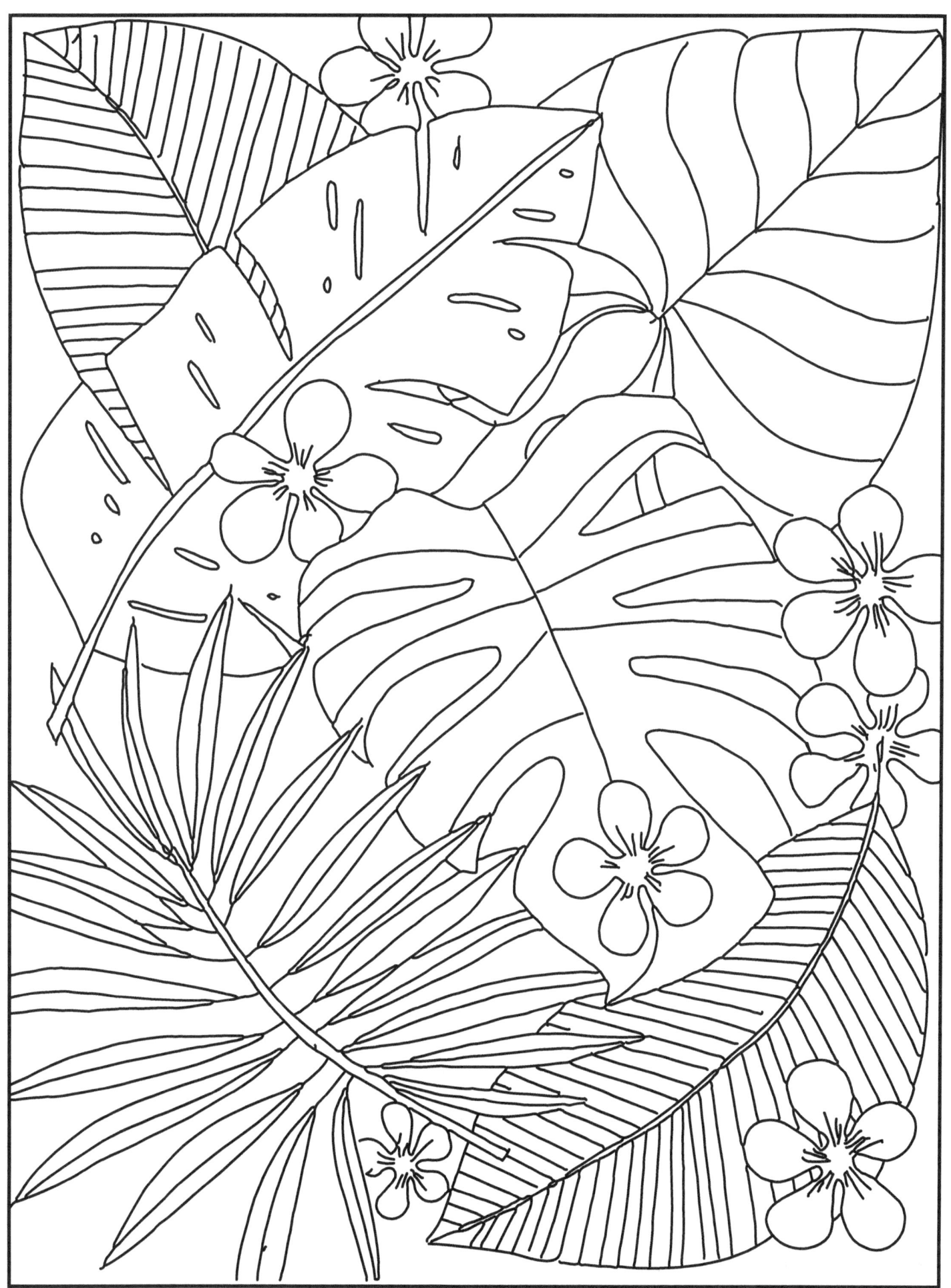

Caribbean Collection - NATURE

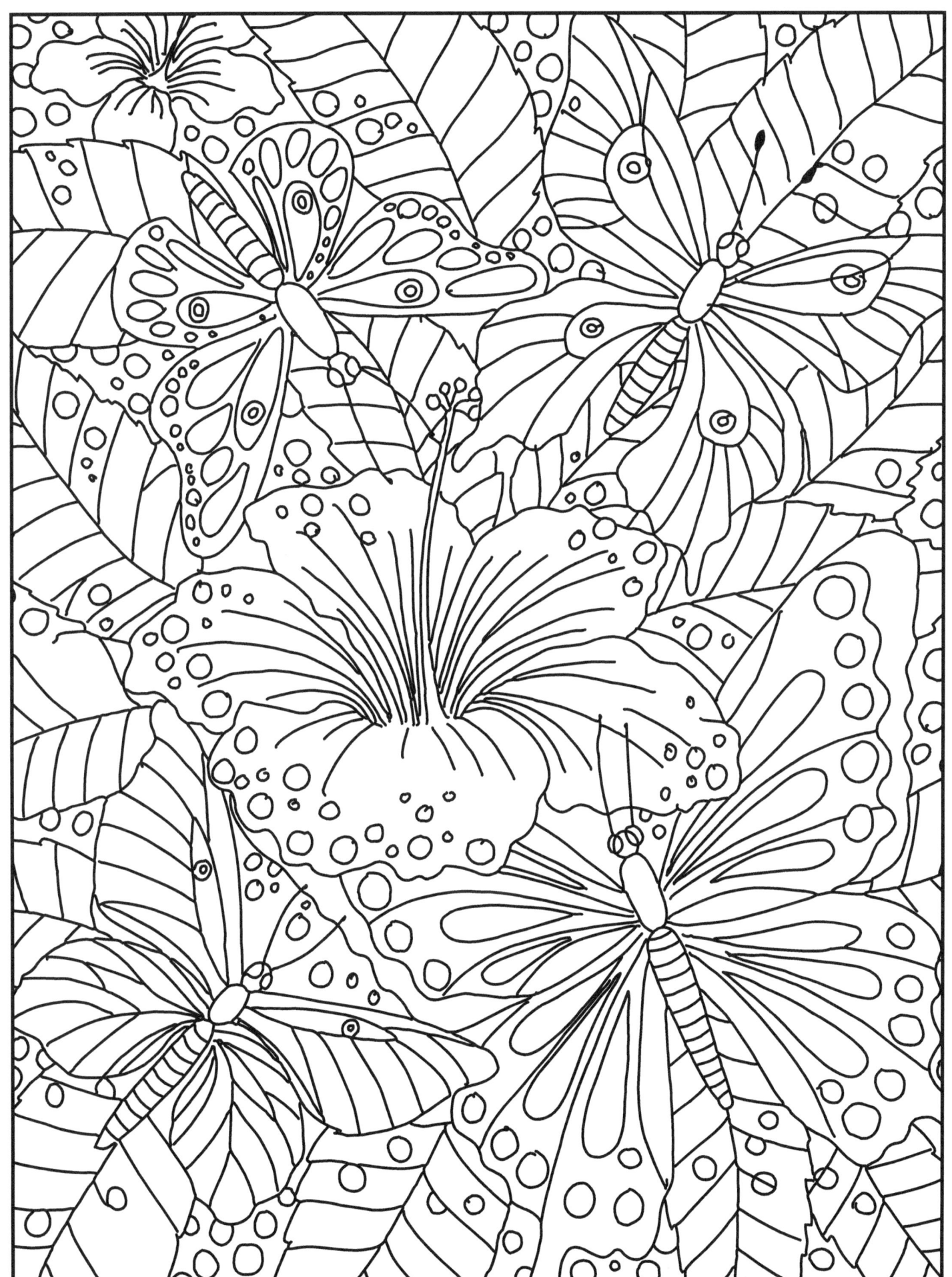

Caribbean Collection - NATURE

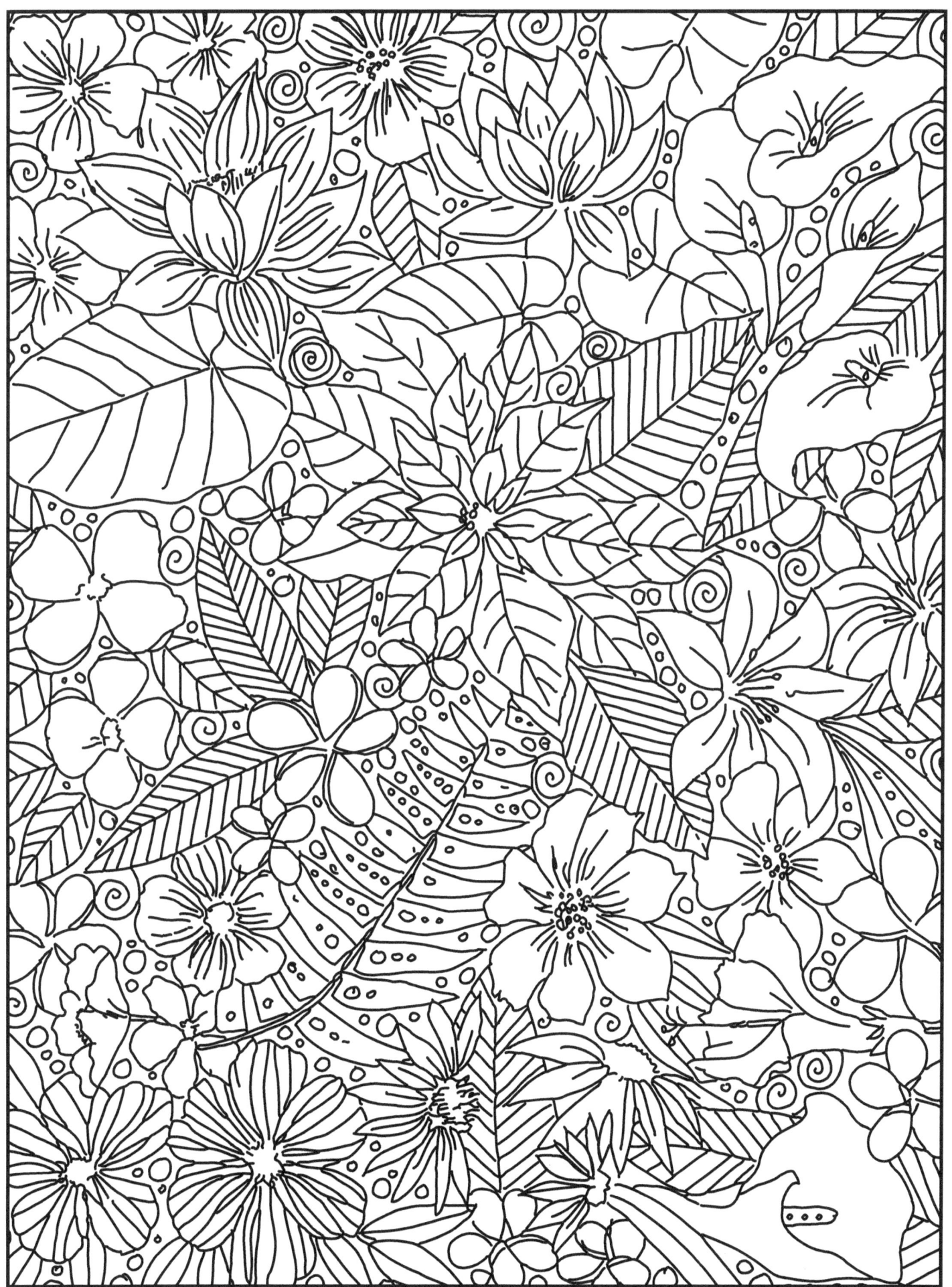

Caribbean Collection - NATURE

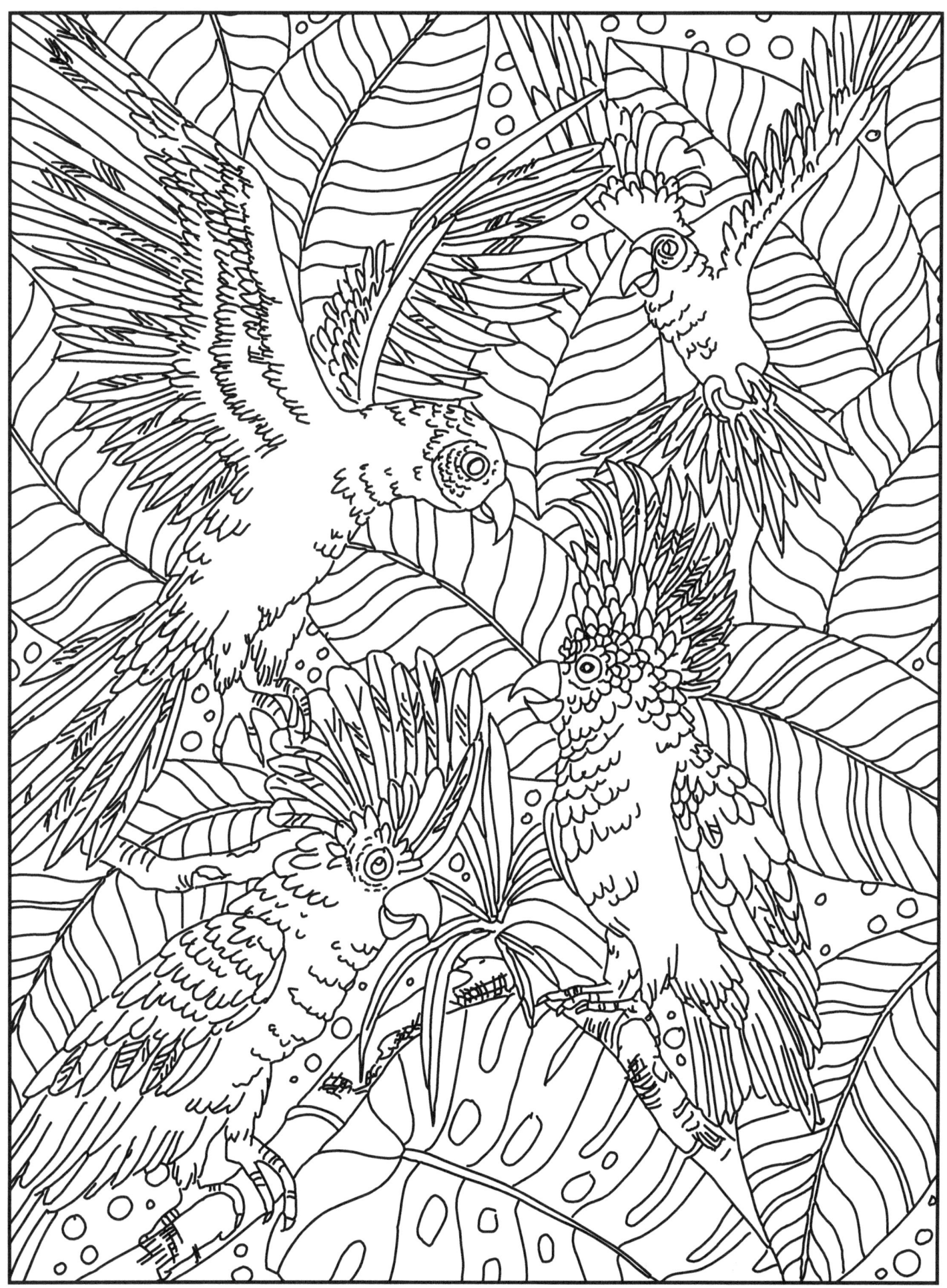

Caribbean Collection - NATURE

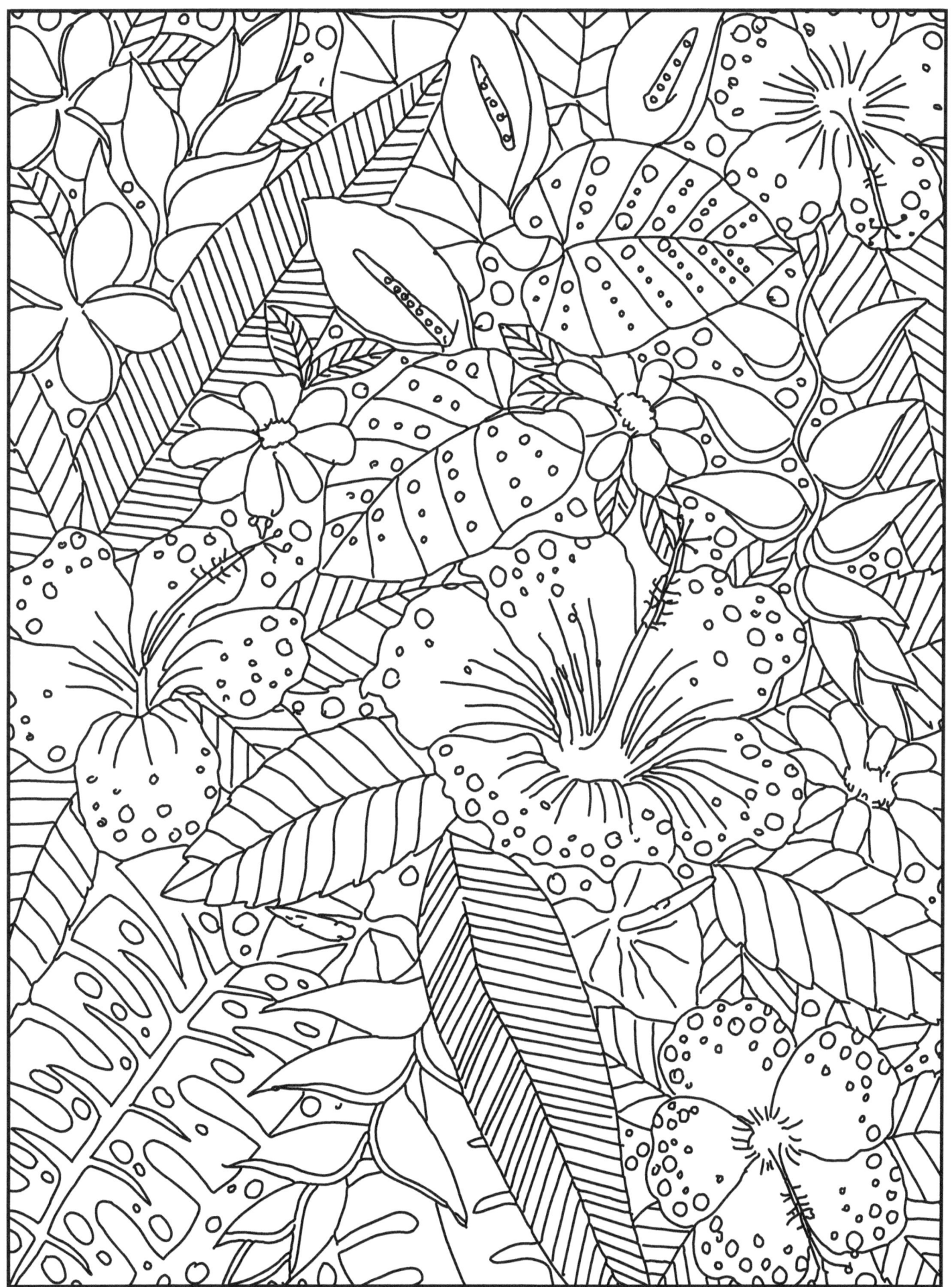

Caribbean Collection - NATURE

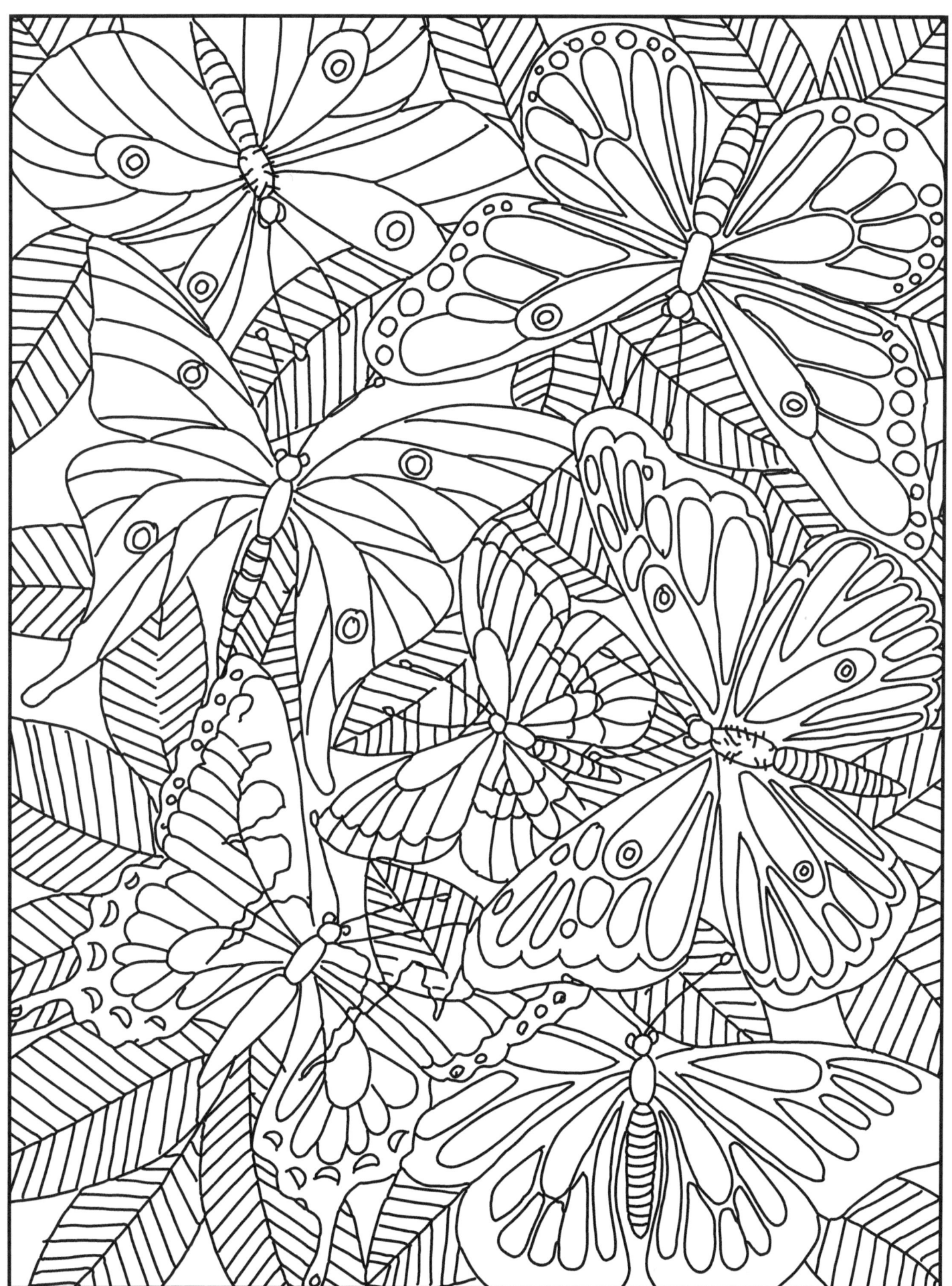

Caribbean Collection - NATURE

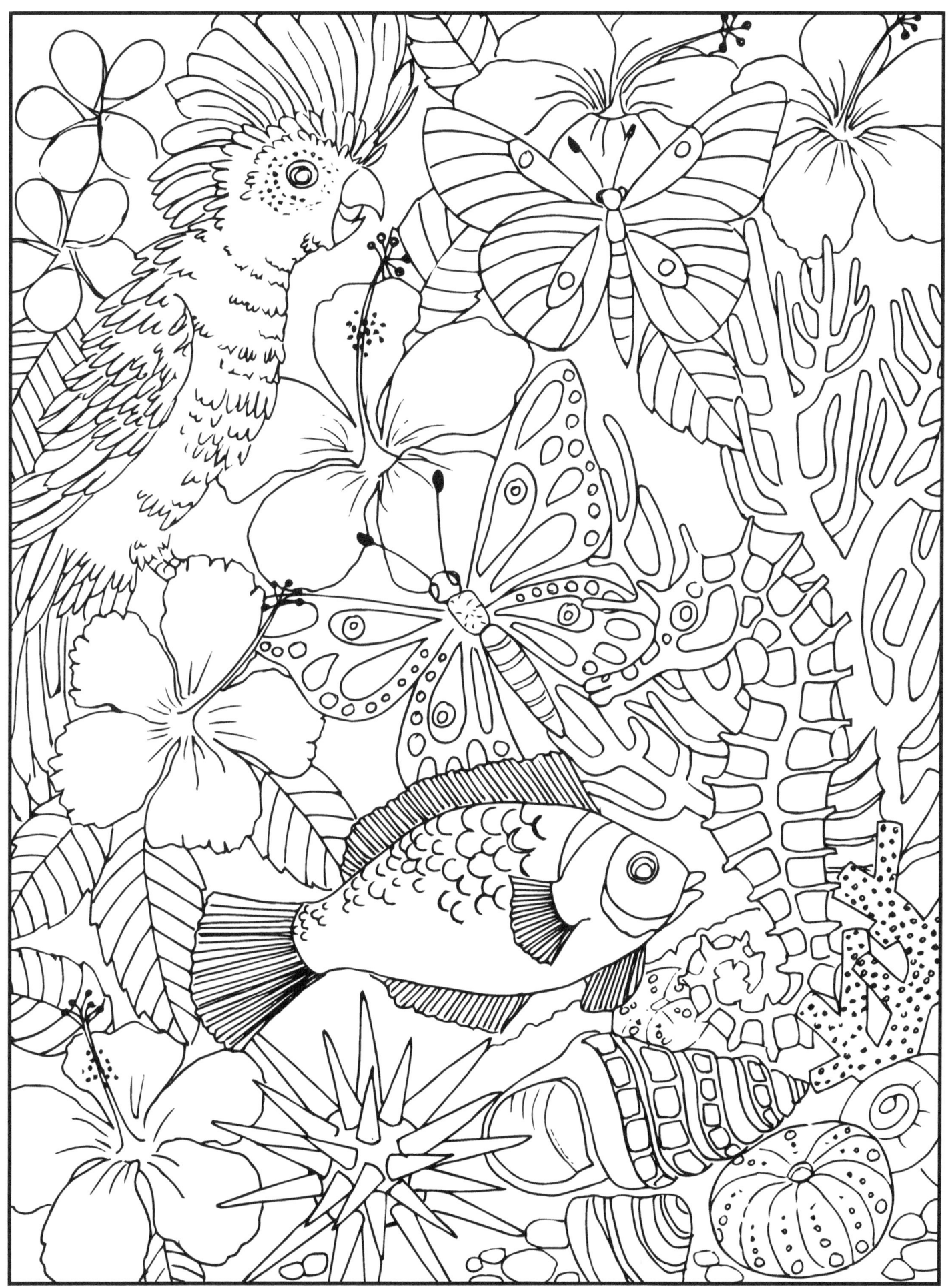

Caribbean Collection - NATURE

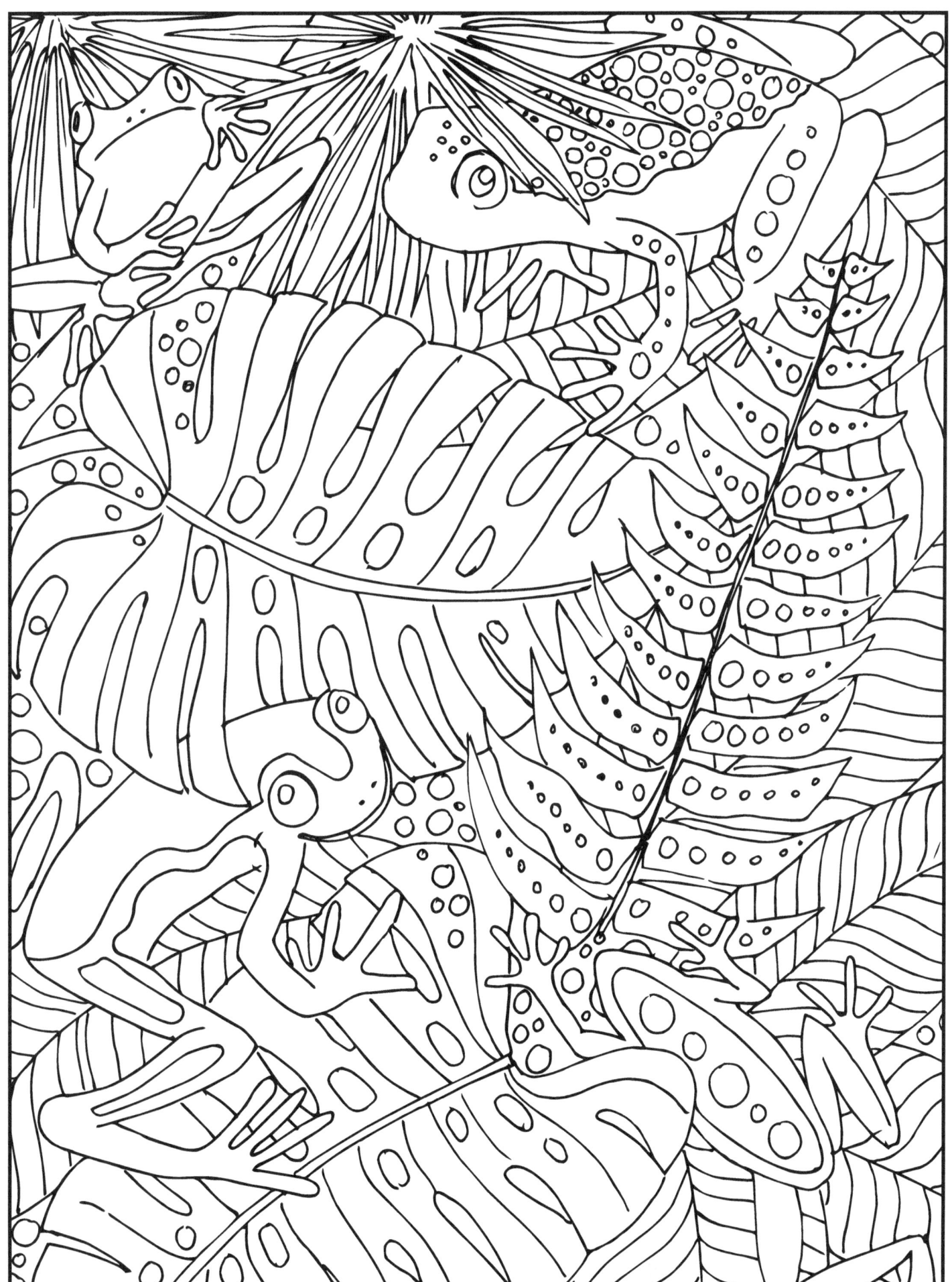

Caribbean Collection - NATURE

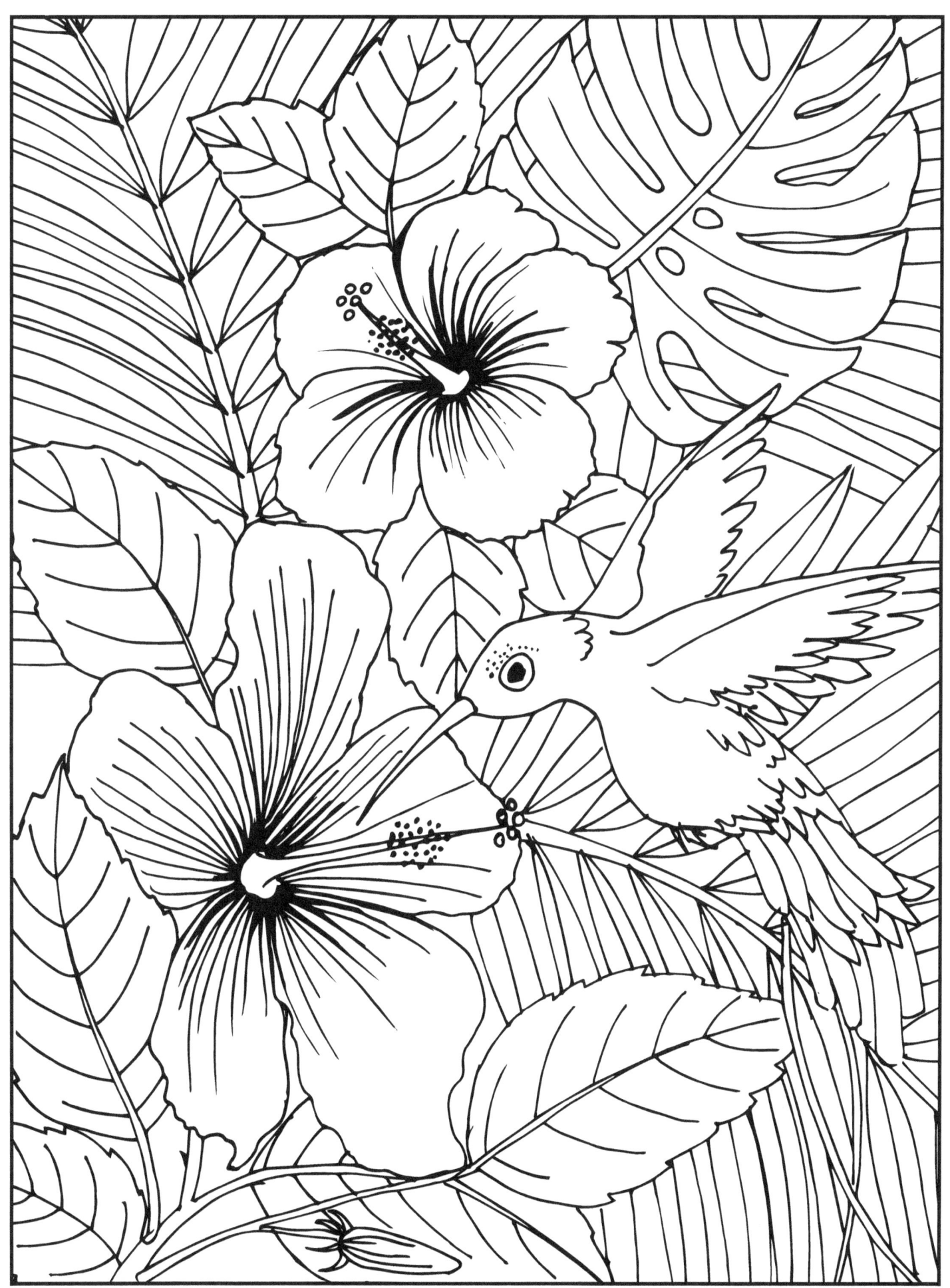

www.ingramcontent.com/pod-product-compliance
Lightning Source LLC
Chambersburg PA
CBHW080629220526
45467CB00011B/3441